RESCUING Animals FROM DISASTERS

SAVING ANIMALS FROM VOLCANOES

by Miriam Aronin

Consultant: Dessy Zahara Angelina Pane
Animal Friends Jogja (AFJ)

BEARPORT
PUBLISHING

New York, New York

Credits

Cover and Title Page, © Adek Berry/AFP/Getty Images and Richard Ustinich/Riser/Getty Images; 4, © Nomad/SuperStock; 5, © Adi Weda/EPA/Landov; 7, © Agus Suparto/AFP/Getty Images; 8, © Dwi Oblo/Reuters/Landov; 9T, © Animal Friends Jogja; 9B, © Jakarta Animal Aid Network; 10, © Dito Yuwono; 11, © Jakarta Animal Aid Network; 12, © Animal Rescue Team Merapi (AFJ, JAAN and COP); 13, © Animal Rescue Team Merapi (AFJ, JAAN and COP); 14, © Animal Friends Jogja; 15L, Courtesy of Karin Franken; 15R, © Animal Rescue Team Merapi (AFJ, JAAN and COP); 16, © Adek Berry/AFP/Getty Images; 16i, © Jakarta Animal Aid Network; 17L, © Jakarta Animal Aid Network; 17R, © Jakarta Animal Aid Network; 18T, © Animal Rescue Team Merapi (AFJ, JAAN and COP); 18B, © Kiswandari Setyawati/Animal Friends Jogja; 19, © Animal Friends Jogja; 20, © Animal Friends Jogja; 21, © Animal Friends Jogja; 22L, © Jakarta Animal Aid Network; 22R, © Animal Rescue Team Merapi (AFJ, JAAN and COP); 23, © Animal Rescue Team Merapi (AFJ, JAAN and COP); 24L, © Clara Prima/AFP/Getty Images; 24R, © Slamet/EPA/Landov; 25T, © Animal Rescue Team Merapi (AFJ, JAAN and COP); 25B, © Animal Rescue Team Merapi (AFJ, JAAN and COP); 26, © Animal Rescue Team Merapi (AFJ, JAAN and COP); 27, Courtesy of Susan Gilbertson; 28, © Ivan Alvarado/Reuters/Landov; 29, © Romeo Ranoco/Reuters/Landov.

Publisher: Kenn Goin
Senior Editor: Lisa Wiseman
Creative Director: Spencer Brinker
Design: Dawn Beard Creative and Kim Jones
Photo Researcher: Mary Fran Loftus

Library of Congress Cataloging-in-Publication Data

Aronin, Miriam.
    Saving animals from volcanoes / by Miriam Aronin.
        p. cm.— (Rescuing animals from disasters)
    Includes bibliographical references and index.
    ISBN-13: 978-1-61772-291-2 (library binding)
    ISBN-10: 1-61772-291-X (library binding)
    1. Animal rescue—Juvenile literature. 2. Animals—Effect of volcanic eruptions on—Juvenile literature.
3. Volcanic eruptions—Juvenile literature. I. Title.
    QL83.2.A76 2012
    639.9—dc22
                                        2011014176

For more information, write to Bearport Publishing Company, Inc., 45 West 21st Street, Suite 3B, New York, New York 10010. Printed in the United States of America in North Mankato, Minnesota.

072011
042711CGF

10 9 8 7 6 5 4 3 2 1

CONTENTS

A Mountain of Fire.................... 4

Land of Volcanoes..................... 6

Helping Out 8

A Dried-Out Forest 10

Starving Monkeys 12

A Dog Named Foxy 14

Pets in Trouble 16

Temporary Houses 18

One More Dog 20

Macaque Rescue 22

Food Trucks.......................... 24

"Some Happy Endings".................. 26

Famous Volcanic Eruptions
and Rescues 28

Animals at Risk from
Volcanic Eruptions 29

Glossary 30

Bibliography 31

Read More 31

Learn More Online 31

Index 32

About the Author...................... 32

A Mountain of Fire

In October 2010, scientists made a frightening discovery. Mount Merapi, a powerful **volcano** on the island of Java in Indonesia, was about to **erupt**. Thousands of farmers, villagers, and animals lived within 15 miles (24 km) of the volcano. Soon their homes would not be safe.

The government began making plans to **evacuate** everyone. "This is high **alert**," warned volcano expert Dr. Surono on October 25.

This school is located near Mount Merapi.

That day, Mount Merapi erupted. Hot gases and **ash** shot 16,400 feet (5,000 m) into the air. People rushed to flee their homes. Many had no time to take their pets and **livestock** with them. Would anyone come rescue the animals?

Before Mount Merapi erupted, very hot liquid rock built up under the ground. It then burst out of an opening in the mountain, along with blasts of hot gas and ash.

Merapi means "mountain of fire" in the Indonesian language.

Land of Volcanoes

Volcanoes such as Mount Merapi have been erupting in Indonesia for thousands of years. In fact, scientists believe that the largest volcanic eruption on Earth happened there about 75,000 years ago. Today, Indonesia has more than 75 **active volcanoes**, more than any other country in the world.

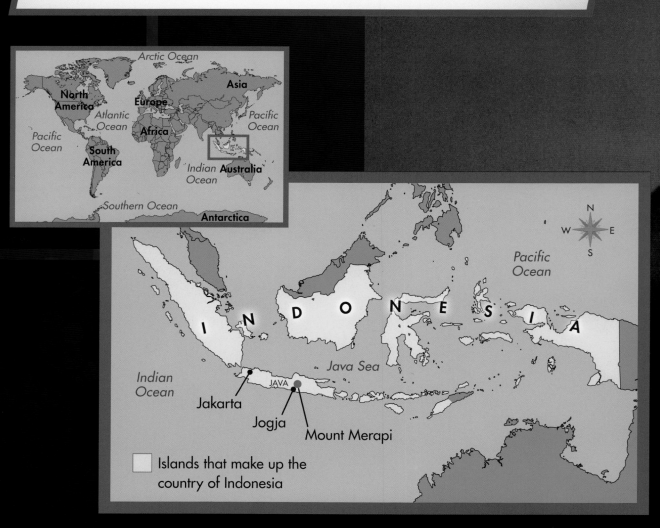

Islands that make up the country of Indonesia

Indonesia is made up of more than 17,500 islands in Southeast Asia. Mount Merapi is on Java, one of the larger islands.

When one of these volcanoes erupts, the result can be deadly for humans and other animals. For example, hot gas and ash can easily fill the lungs and make it difficult for the victims of the volcano to breathe. When plants that many animals depend on for food are killed by hot **lava** and ash, the animals face starvation.

Mount Merapi erupting in 2006

Though no one knows for sure, scientists believe that volcanoes have erupted in Indonesia more than 1,100 times since the third century A.D. Mount Merapi erupts about every four years.

Helping Out

When Mount Merapi began erupting in 2010, animal rescue groups were worried. Many animals lived near the volcano. What would happen to them?

On October 27, 2010, **volunteers** came together to form the Merapi Animal Rescue Team. Their goal was to help save the animals that were in danger of being killed by the erupting volcano. The team set up a base camp in Yogyakarta, also called Jogja, a city near Mount Merapi. The rescue team planned to live at the base camp and bring any animals injured by the eruption there for medical treatment.

The

The 25-member team was made up of **veterinarians**, experienced animal handlers, and animal rescue workers. One of the volunteers, Femke den Haas, traveled 275 miles (443 km) from her home in the city of Jakarta to join the rescue team in Jogja. Though team members would be working in dangerous conditions, they were determined to save the animals threatened by the eruption.

Part of the Merapi Animal Rescue Team

The Merapi Animal Rescue Team was made up of volunteers from three animal protection groups—the Jakarta Animal Aid Network (JAAN), the Center for Orangutan Protection (COP), and Animal Friends Jogja (AFJ).

Femke helped create JAAN in 2008.

9

A Dried-Out Forest

On October 30, a few days after arriving in Jogja, the rescue team went to the Tlogo Putri mountain **resort** area, which is located only two and a half miles (4 km) from the top of Mount Merapi. The team wanted to check on monkeys called long-tailed **macaques** that made their homes in trees there. They were worried that the animals might be starving or injured as a result of the eruption.

The volcanic eruption destroyed this road leading to the resort, making it hard for rescuers to get there.

The Tlogo Putri mountain resort area had been part of a beautiful forest before the eruption in 2010. **Tourists** often visited the area and fed the monkeys. When Mount Merapi erupted, however, it blasted the trees and other plants with hot air and ashes. Instead of finding a green, leafy forest, the team saw a shocking sight. "The forest is now completely dry," said Femke. "The trees are cracking from the heat."

Although the team found some macaques that were still alive, though starving, they also found the bodies of two monkeys. The terrible heat from the volcano had killed them.

Members of the rescue team looking for macaques that survived the eruption

Heat and ash from volcanoes can be deadly for animals. Some scientists believe that volcanic eruptions are one reason that dinosaurs became extinct.

Starving Monkeys

After finding the dead macaques, the rescue team continued to return to Tlogo Putri from their base camp. The rescuers found more monkeys that were starving. The volcano had killed much of the plant life in the forest, which the animals depended on for food. Also, since the eruption forced the resort to close, there were no tourists to feed the animals.

These monkeys survived the eruption.

The rescuers went to Tlogo Putri every day for about two months to help the monkeys. To regain their strength, the monkeys needed lots of fruits and vegetables. Luckily, the rescue team received food donations from Jogja supermarkets. They were given fruit and vegetables that were damaged and couldn't be sold. Every night the rescuers sorted through the food and removed the rotten pieces and then washed what could still be eaten.

After its first eruption at the end of October, Mount Merapi erupted several more times. An area around the volcano was declared a **danger zone** by the Indonesian government. This meant that the area was unsafe because the volcano was in danger of erupting. Most people were not allowed inside this area. The rescue team, however, had special **permits** from the government to enter the danger zone.

This macaque is eating a piece of fruit provided by the rescue team. Rescuers brought nuts, yams, sweet potatoes carrots, bananas, and cucumbers to the hungry macaques.

A Dog Named Foxy

One day while feeding the macaques in Tlogo Putri, the rescue team spotted a little female dog that appeared to be sick. Everyone on the team wanted to help her, but the volcano had just released a hot ash cloud, called a **pyroclastic flow**. If the rescuers didn't leave immediately, they faced serious harm. One of the rescuers decided to scoop up the small dog as the team headed back to base camp. Once there, the little dog got a name—Foxy.

A rescuer with Foxy

Pyroclastic flows, which are made up of hot ash and poisonous gases, can be deadly. If caught in one, a person can be badly burned or choke to death.

Karin Franken, a member of JAAN, said the small dog "was pitiful to see." No one had fed Foxy for more than a week, so she was very thin. She also had **parasites** and a **tumor** in her stomach.

Fortunately, members of the rescue team had sent for a veterinarian from Jakarta. The vet performed surgery on the dog to remove the tumor and provided medicine to get rid of the parasites. Then a volunteer in Jakarta took care of Foxy while she recovered.

Karin Franken helped Foxy and other dogs after the eruption of Mount Merapi.

Foxy after being rescued

Pets in Trouble

Foxy was not the only dog that needed help. Many people who fled from their homes when the volcano erupted had to leave their pets behind. As rescuers searched empty villages for **abandoned** animals, they found dogs, rabbits, cats, and birds.

This village was destroyed by the hot gas and ash from the volcano.

Rescuers looked for animals that survived the eruption in villages covered with volcanic ash.

Just like the wild monkeys in Tlogo Putri, the abandoned pets needed food. The rescuers fed and cared for them in the villages until their owners could return.

Many of the animals the rescuers found were not only hungry, but also injured. Some had burns from the hot volcanic ash and others had damaged lungs from breathing it in. These injured animals were taken back to the base camp, where they received medical care.

These rescuers found caged birds.

A rabbit that was left behind by its owners being cared for by a volunteer

Ash from the volcano affected animals as far away as Jogja, which is about 20 miles (32 km) from Mount Merapi. At the Center for Orangutan Protection in Jogja, workers put masks on the orangutans to protect them from breathing in ash.

Temporary Houses

Back at the base camp, the injured and sick animals lived in **temporary** cages. Volunteers gave them **antibiotics** and vitamins to help them get better. To treat the ones with burns, volunteers rubbed **ointment** onto the animals' skin to help them heal.

These rescuers are bringing a dog named Maya to their base camp.

Rescuers found this kitten trapped in a destroyed house in a small village called Dusun Kinahrejo. She was having trouble breathing due to the thick ash that covered the village. The rescuers named her Merina. They took her back to Jogja to give her medical treatment.

As the health of the animals improved, they were allowed to move around outside their cages. Soon the healthy cats were moved from the camp to a nearby house owned by members of Animal Friends Jogja (AFJ). It was, however, not large enough to house the dogs, too.

Fortunately, in late November, a kind person lent AFJ another house near Jogja. It was a perfect home for the dogs, because it had a yard where they could move around. It also had enough space indoors for all the injured dogs. Two veterinarians stayed at the house to give the animals medical care.

This is the house where the dogs lived.

Volunteers walked the dogs living in the AFJ house twice a day, along with help from local children

One More Dog

On December 4, 2010, the rescuers went to Petung **Hamlet**. The tiny town had been destroyed by hot gas and ash from the volcano. A journalist, who was writing an article about the devastation, had told the rescuers about the town's only survivor—a dog living in a burnt-down house. When the rescuers found the dog, he had painful burns all over his body. His throat was sore, and he had trouble barking. He was also very hungry.

Petung Hamlet's lone survivor with his rescuers

The rescuers named the dog Rocky, gave him some food, and then loaded him onto a **motorbike**. They drove him to the AFJ house where the veterinarians treated him. Soon, Rocky's throat and burns began to heal.

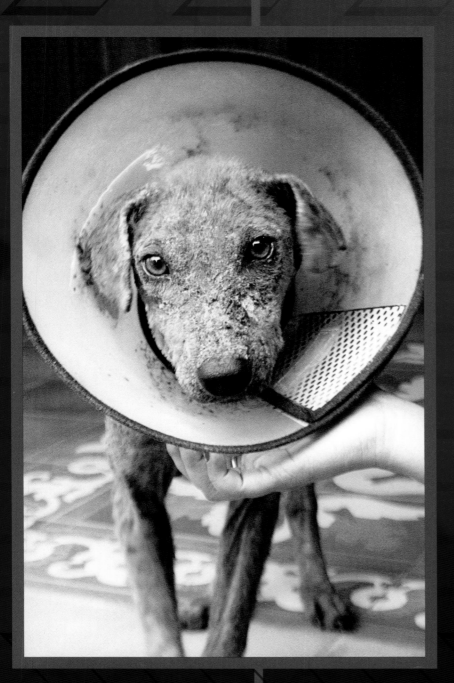

Rocky had to wear a special collar to keep him from licking his burnt skin.

Some villages near the volcano, such as Petung Hamlet, were buried under up to 12 inches (30 cm) of ash.

Macaque Rescue

Cats and dogs were not the only pets that rescuers found in the abandoned villages. They also discovered macaques that people had kept chained up in cages. After being left alone for many days, the monkeys were hungry and thirsty. That was not their only problem, however.

Macaques are wild, powerful animals. They shouldn't be locked up in cages like pets. The monkeys need to be in a place where they can live freely. Moving macaques can be tricky, however. They often get scared and attack the people moving them.

Rescuers found this macaque chained up in a cage.

Rescuers discuss how to move the macaques to a safe place.

To keep everyone safe, rescuers shot the macaques with **anesthetic** darts. The darts contained drugs that put the monkeys to sleep without hurting them.

The rescuers then transported the monkeys to the base camp in cars and pickup trucks. Later, after a medical check, team members took the macaques to an animal rescue center in west Java. There, they would learn to live in the wild.

Rescuers use anesthetic darts to make the macaques fall asleep before moving them to the rescue center.

Adult long-tailed macaques are between 15 and 26 inches (38 and 66 cm) tall. They weigh between 5.5 and 18.3 pounds (2.5 and 8.3 kg). Males are larger and heavier than females.

Food Trucks

Besides pets and wild animals, the rescuers also helped save farm animals. When the eruption started, many farmers had to leave their livestock, such as **cattle**, behind. There was no time to move them.

Normally, cattle eat grass. However, after the eruption, ash from the volcano covered the grass, making it unsafe to eat. Also, because it was still too dangerous to return to their farms, the farmers weren't able to bring clean grass to their cattle. How would these animals get food?

Besides needing food to eat, many of the cows left behind needed medical care because they suffered from severe burns.

Before the eruption began, farmers were raising about 3,000 cattle on the slopes of Mount Merapi.

Farmers who lived farther away from the volcano helped. Some sold grass from their fields to the rescuers. Others agreed to give them the corn leaves from their **crops**. The team cut the leaves themselves and loaded them onto pickup trucks. The rescuers hauled two or three full loads to the starving cattle every day.

Members of the Merapi Animal Rescue Team brought clean food and water to the cattle.

Volunteers cut corn leaves and grasses for the cattle to eat.

"Some Happy Endings"

After the volcano erupted, rescuers stayed in the area for more than six weeks to help nearby animals. In total, they took food to 60 macaques, more than 200 dogs, and countless cats. They also fed at least 400 chickens, 25 rabbits, 85 ducks, and 3 geese. They trucked in grass for more than 40 cows.

A veterinarian treating a dog rescued after the eruption

About 390,000 people were evacuated from their homes to temporary camps around Jogja. Many of these people's homes and farms were destroyed in the 2010 eruption of Mount Merapi.

After about six weeks, it was finally safe for people to return to their homes. They would now be able to take care of their pets and livestock.

Karin from JAAN helped some animals without owners find new homes. For example, Foxy was **adopted** by a woman named Susan Gilbertson in Jakarta. "It's good to have some happy endings," said Karin.

Foxy in her new home

FAMOUS VOLCANIC ERUPTIONS AND RESCUES

Rescue workers have learned a lot from rescuing animals after volcanic eruptions. Here are two other eruptions that put animals in danger.

Soufrière Hills Volcano, Montserrat, 1997

- The Soufrière Hills volcano on the island of Montserrat erupted on June 25, 1997. People fleeing from the area left behind about 300 pets and several hundred farm animals. After the eruption, many of the animals were in poor health. They didn't have enough to eat. Some had burns on their bodies. Ash from the volcano had damaged some of their teeth. There were some dogs that could no longer bark after breathing in the hot gas.

- Rescuers from the World Society for the Protection of Animals treated the injured animals. Then they moved the farm animals to a nearby island. They put the pets on ships and airplanes to Florida. There, the animals found new homes with American families.

Chaitén Volcano, Chile, 2008

- The Chaitén volcano in Chile erupted on May 2, 2008. People fleeing from the area left behind about 4,000 pets and 50,000 farm animals. These animals had little clean food or water. There were so many abandoned dogs that reporters called Chaitén "a city taken by dogs."

- Rescuers from groups such as the Humane Society of the United States, Humane Society International, and International Fund for Animal Welfare evacuated more than 100 dogs. They brought food, water, and medicine to many animals. When people could return to the area, rescuers helped many families find their lost pets.

This dog was rescued after the earthquake in Chaitén, Chile.

ANIMALS AT RISK FROM VOLCANIC ERUPTIONS

Volcanic eruptions are dangerous natural disasters that can affect several different kinds of animals.

Pets, Wild Animals, and Livestock

- Pets, wild animals, and livestock can all be burned by very hot gas, ash, or lava during a volcanic eruption. Pets that are tied up or kept in cages cannot escape the heat.

- When an area is damaged by hot ash and lava, pet owners and farmers cannot return home to care for their animals until the area becomes safe again. These abandoned animals need food and clean water to survive.

- Hot gas and ash can kill plants and make fresh water dirty. Without help, pets, wild animals, and livestock may die from hunger or thirst.

A rescue worker trying to get a water buffalo on a truck after a volcanic eruption in the Philippines in 2009

Sea Creatures

- When hot volcanic lava, ash, and gas flow into the ocean, they can be deadly for creatures such as fish, seals, and birds.

- The heat from the lava, ash, and gas can make ocean water so hot that it boils. Fish cannot survive in such high temperatures. The heat may burn other animals that try to enter the water, such as seals and birds, as well.

GLOSSARY

abandoned (uh-BAN-duhnd) left alone, without help

active volcanoes (AK-tiv vol-KAY-nohz) volcanoes that release gas and lava, even in small amounts

adopted (uh-DOPT-id) taken in as part of a family

alert (uh-LURT) a warning of danger

anesthetic (an-iss-THET-ik) a drug given to people or animals to prevent them from feeling any pain

antibiotics (*an*-ti-bye-OT-iks) medicines used to destroy or stop the growth of bacteria that cause diseases

ash (ASH) tiny volcanic pieces of rock and minerals

cattle (KAT-uhl) cows, bulls, and similar animals raised on a farm

crops (KROPS) plants that are grown and gathered, often for food

danger zone (DAYN-jur ZOHN) an area that has been declared unsafe

erupt (i-RUPT) to send out lava, ash, steam, and gas from a volcano

evacuate (i-VAK-yoo-*ate*) to remove from a dangerous area

extinct (ek-STINGKT) no longer existing

hamlet (HAM-lit) a tiny village

lava (LAH-vuh) hot liquid rock that comes out of a volcano

livestock (LIVE-*stok*) animals raised on a farm or ranch, such as horses, sheep, and cows

macaques (muh-KAHKS) a large group of monkeys found mostly in southern Asia; some have long tails while others have short or no tails at all

motorbike (MOH-tur-*bike*) a small, light motorcycle

ointment (OINT-muhnt) a thick, sometimes greasy substance that is put on the skin to heal or protect it

parasites (PA-ruh-*sites*) plants or animals that get food by living on or in another plant or animal, sometimes making that plant or animal sick

permits (PUR-mits) documents giving permission to do something

pyroclastic flow (*pye*-roh-KLAS-tik FLOH) a fast-moving cloud of hot ash and deadly gases, often part of a volcanic eruption

resort (ri-ZORT) a place where tourists relax and have fun

temporary (TEM-puh-*rer*-ee) lasting for a short period of time; not permanent

tourists (TOOR-ists) people who travel and visit places for fun

tumor (TOO-mur) an unusual lump or growth in the body

veterinarians (*vet*-ur-uh-NAIR-ee-uhnz) doctors who take care of dogs and other animals

volcano (vol-KAY-noh) an opening in the Earth's surface from which melted rock or ash can shoot out

volunteers (*vol*-uhn-TIHRZ) people who offer to do a job without pay

BIBLIOGRAPHY

The Bali Times. "Animal Lovers Bandy Together to Save Merapi Wildlife" (November 8, 2010).
www.thebalitimes.com/2010/11/08/
animal-lovers-bandy-together-to-save-merapi-wildlife/

Figge, Katrin. "Rescue for Merapi's Furry Survivors." *Jakarta Globe* (November 8, 2010).
www.thejakartaglobe.com/lifeandtimes/
rescue-for-merapis-furry-survivors/405547

Kegel, Maria L. "Animals Need Rescuing Too." *The Jakarta Post* (December 15, 2010).
www.thejakartapost.com/news/2010/12/15/animals-need-rescuing-too.html

Kegel, Maria L. "Volcano Dogs Arrive in Jakarta for a Happy Ending." *The Jakarta Post* (December 15, 2010).
www.thejakartapost.com/news/2010/12/15/
volcano-dogs-arrive-jakarta-a-happy-ending.html

READ MORE

Person, Stephen. *Devastated by a Volcano! (Disaster Survivors).* New York: Bearport (2010).

Riley, Gail Blasser. *Volcano! The 1980 Mount St. Helens Eruption (X-treme Disasters that Changed America).* New York: Bearport (2006).

Woods, Michael and Mary B. *Volcanoes.* Minneapolis, MN: Lerner (2007).

LEARN MORE ONLINE

To learn more about saving animals from volcanic eruptions, visit
www.bearportpublishing.com/RescuingAnimalsfromDisasters

INDEX

Animal Friends Jogja (AFJ) 9, 19, 21

antibiotics 18

ash 5, 7, 11, 14, 16–17, 18, 20–21, 24, 28–29

burns 17, 18, 20–21, 24, 28–29

cats 16, 19, 22, 26

cattle 24–25

Center for Orangutan Protection (COP) 9, 17

chickens 26

Chile 28

danger zone 13

den Haas, Femke 9, 11

dogs 14–15, 16, 18–19, 20–21, 22, 26, 28

farmers 4, 24–25

Foxy 14–15, 16, 27

Franken, Karin 15, 27

Gilbertson, Susan 27

grass 24–25, 26

Indonesia 4–5, 6–7

Jakarta 9, 15, 27

Jakarta Animal Aid Network (JAAN) 9, 15, 27

Jogja 8–9, 13, 17, 18–19, 26

livestock 5, 24, 27, 29

macaques 10–11, 12–13, 14, 22–23, 26

Montserrat 28

orangutans 9, 17

pets 5, 8, 16–17, 22, 24, 27, 28–29

Petung Hamlet 20–21

Rocky 20–21

Surono, Dr. 4

Tlogo Putri 10–11, 12, 14, 17

veterinarians 9, 15, 19, 21

volunteers 8–9, 15, 17, 18–19, 25

ABOUT THE AUTHOR

Miriam Aronin is a writer and editor. She also enjoys reading, dancing, knitting, and playing with her friends' pets.